TENNIS
NOTES

TENNIS NOTES

JAMES WAGENVOORD

ST. MARTIN'S PRESS

For information, write:
St. Martin's Press
175 Fifth Avenue
New York, N.Y. 10010

The Official Rules of Tennis, pp 58-61, © 1980
The United States Tennis Association, Inc.

Created and produced by James Wagenvoord Studio, Inc.
Editor: James Wagenvoord
Senior Editor: Dinah Stevenson
Assistant Editor: Anne Dodd
Design: Marta Norman
Assisting in the creation of this book:
Fiona St. Aubyn, Shawn Hancock, Dewey Thompson,
Elizabeth Goldwyn, Marie G. Dodd, Cory Alperstein

Published by St. Martin's Press
New York

Manufactured in the United States of America
First printing
ISBN 0-312-79104-6

CONTENTS

HOW TO USE
THIS BOOK

TENNIS NOTES consists of a number of brief, informative sections designed to increase your working knowledge and understanding of the game. You will learn something about the unusual history of tennis, about the basics of scoring and tournament play, and about the important, though often unspoken, rules of court etiquette.

This book also covers developments and innovations in the construction and design of racquets, and describes the different court surfaces and the characteristics of each. There is also information about a new national program for evaluating your tennis skills.

Most important, this book can show you that learning about tennis is an integral part of playing tennis and of developing a better and more sophisticated game. There is advice on finding a teacher and on what you can expect once you have found one, suggestions for things you can do to get the most out of a lesson, and some techniques for practicing, and using, what you have learned.

Most of the book is designed for you to use regularly, even daily, to keep track of your tennis progress. The *Lesson Log* can be used to record the tips and suggestions of your tennis pro for quick and easy reference. Going back over these important points can help prevent you from simply reverting to old and bad habits when you practice. With the Lesson Log you'll get the most our of your lessons and the most out of yourself.

The *Tennis Log* section provides a single, convenient place to note your tennis commitments from week to week. In the *Match Log* you can record the results of each match and note points for future concentration and practice. With the *Tournament Log* you can keep a record of your competitive tennis play.

Using the *Equipment Expense Log* you can keep track of your inventory of tennis paraphernalia. It will also serve as a reference for such important things as when you last had your racquet strung, and where you found that particularly effective leather grip. It will also help provide an accounting of your tennis expenses. When you have recorded all the important phone numbers in *Tennis Names and Numbers,* a friendly or competitive game or some advice from a tennis pro will be only a quick phone call away.

TENNIS NOTES should become a permanent personal resource, something you can use to refine your tennis skills and increase your appreciation of the game.

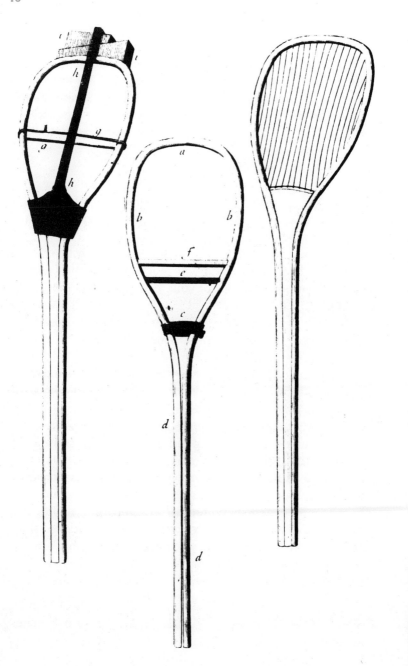

EQUIPMENT
&
COURT BASICS

You don't need very much equipment to play tennis. The basic requirements are simple – a racquet, some tennis balls, tennis shoes, and an empty court (which may be the most difficult thing to find). But the variety of different types of equipment can be overwhelming. Some simple shopping and buying advice from a tennis professional can be very helpful and can save you time, money, and frustration.

THE RACQUET

The racquet is the most important piece of equipment. It should be carefully selected to conform to your own style of play as well as to the size of your body and hand. Most important, you should pick a racquet that simply feels right.

There are no official specifications for the size and weight of a tennis racquet. Each make of racquet comes with varying grip sizes, as well as differing combinations of weight and balance.

GRIPS

The grip is measured in the middle of the handle. The handle, generally either octagonal or rounded, is covered with calfskin or cowhide, although vinyl is sometimes used. The smallest standard-sized grip is 4½ inches around, and the largest is 4⅞ inches, with other sizes at intervals of ⅛ inch. Some smaller racquets for junior players measure 4 inches around, while others for some tennis pros measure 5 inches.

Obviously, the smaller your hand, the smaller your grip size will be. Some, however, prefer to play with racquets normally considered too small or too large.

FRAMES

The lightest racquets, measured without strings, weigh between 12 and 12¾ ounces. Medium-sized racquets weigh from 12½ to 13½ ounces. Heavy racquets weigh from 13½ to 14¾ ounces, and extra-heavy racquets weigh more than 14¾ ounces. Again, the weight of the racquet you select should be based on your individual preference and strength. A physically strong player can use a heavy frame which can give more momentum to the swing. Players with limited upper-body strength often prefer a lighter racquet.

Racquets are also balanced differently and should be selected by how they feel in your hand. Try a racquet out on the court if possible. As measured from the center, a racquet can be even-balanced, head-light, or head-heavy. Most professionals prefer a head-light racquet because it helps them put more spin on the ball.

RACQUET TYPES

There are five basic types of racquet: wood, steel, aluminum, fiberglass, and composites (which include combinations of various materials such as epoxy and graphite). Each racquet type has characteristics which may or may not suit your personal taste and style of play. The prices of each also vary tremendously. Continuing development of new racquet materials and technologies means that still other types of racquets are bound to enter the market.

Wood. All tennis racquets were wood until a little more than ten years ago. The earliest racquets were made from a single piece of wood that was bent to the proper shape. Modern wood racquets are instead made from many thin wood strips called laminates. These extend from the handle around the head and back, and are glued together. Between five and thirteen of these laminates, which are mostly ash, maple, birch, or bamboo, are used. Other layers of wood are often laminated on top of these for added strength or decoration. Fiberglass is also used for an outer coating.

More wood racquets are sold than any other kind. This may be due, in part, to the relatively low cost for a quality racquet. By its very nature, a wood racquet tends to be stiff. It does not flex as much when it strikes the ball as does a metal, fiberglass, or composite racquet. As a result, the wood racquet offers a player less power, but more control.

Steel. The first nonwood racquet was introduced in 1967. It was made of a single piece of steel tubing bent to form the handle and the head, which tends to be rounder than that of a wooden racquet. The curvature of the tube creates an open space at the throat, which is closed with either another piece of tubing or a piece of material called a yoke. The leather grip is built upon pieces of plastic or foam. Durable and much more flexible than wood racquets, steel racquets are among the most powerful, while offering the least control. Although the use of steel for racquet-making has diminished since its original successful introduction, it did lead to further developments in racquet technology.

Aluminum. Aluminum, a very light element, has become the second most popular construction material for tennis racquets. The racquet is formed from a single strip of aluminum alloy, (a combination of aluminum with other elements such as silicon, magnesium, or chromium). This strip is then bent to form the handle and head. A yoke, made of fiberglass or other material, is mounted at the throat and a plastic strip is added around the edge to protect the strings. Although aluminum is lighter than steel, the two types of racquets weigh about the same.

Aluminum racquets are generally stiffer and provide more control than steel. In addition, this stiffness can be tightly controlled, depending upon the specific alloy used.

One of the most recent innovations has been the Large Frame racquet. This aluminum racquet has a significantly larger head than most, providing a 50 percent larger hitting area.

Fiberglass. Fiberglass racquets have become one of the most popular types of racquets used in the tennis industry. The use of fiberglass is similar to applications in other recreational areas, especially skiing. These racquets are molded in one piece and most are of the open-throat design. The tube of a typical racquet is hollow in order to reduce its weight. These racquets tend to be very flexible.

Composite. Composite racquets are composed of a combination of several different materials, each offering special characteristics. Composite racquets are the newest entries in the field and tend to be the most expensive. The racquet is formed from a sandwich of materials molded together. Foam, for example, is often used in the middle, between layers of aluminum or fiberglass. Wood is one of the materials frequently used in the sandwich. Graphite, boron, and other space age materials also can provide strength while adding minimal weight. Most of the composite racquets are of the open-throat design.

STRINGS

There are two choices for stringing your racquet: animal gut or manmade nylon. Each type of string can be installed at a different tension, measured in pounds per inch, from 55 to 65 pounds. In general, the lower the pressure, the more control you can expect.

Gut. Gut strings are made from parts of the intestinal tissue of lambs, sheep, or cattle. Professionals often use gut because of its superior overall playing characteristics. But gut can be easily damaged and is susceptible to dampness and extreme temperature changes. It is also expensive. Gut comes in clear or colored strands which can be combined to form a twist pattern.

Nylon. Nylon strings are more durable than gut and less expensive. They are recommended for average players. The most inexpensive form of nylon – monofilament – contains only a single strand of the fiber and is used mainly on the cheaper, prestrung racquets. Multifilament nylon is considerably more durable and may contain from five to one thousand separate strands of nylon. There have been attempts to manufacture a synthetic gut, out of nylon, which would offer the playing characteristics of gut and the durability of nylon.

THE BALL

The first tennis balls were made of leather and filled with either animal or human hair or poultry feathers. Today, because they are subjected to extreme forces, balls are the only item of equipment for which there is an official USTA standard for construction and performance. Approved balls for competitive play must be yellow or white and must be of an exact size and weight. They also must bounce between 53 and 58 inches when dropped on a concrete surface from exactly 100 inches. The modern tennis ball consists of a rubber sphere covered with a felt "nap," comprised of a blend of nylon, cotton, and wool. The inner sphere normally contains air under pressure to provide a livelier bounce. This pressure gradually diminishes and the ball becomes "dead." Some balls, however, are not pressurized and are designed to last longer, though they tend to be heavier and slower.

Tennis balls are also specifically designed for use on particular surfaces. "Championship" balls are softer and are made for use on clay courts and grass. Heavy-duty balls have more "fuzz" and will last longer in fast play on hard courts.

THE COURTS

The size and shape of a tennis court have not changed since the late 1880s. Today, however, there are a number of different court surfaces. One basic difference between court surfaces is the amount of maintenance; some require almost daily attention, while others need only an occasional resurfacing. Some surfaces are considered "fast," which means that the ball meets little resistance and moves on quickly. Other surfaces provide a resistance which slows the ball, producing a "slow" game.

GRASS

A grass court must be carefully constructed and requires daily care. The bounce on a grass court can be irregular unless the court is in perfect condition. The courts also require a lengthy period to dry after a rain. Considered the most luxurious of all surfaces, grass courts are easy on the feet, beautiful to look at, and generally are thought to be "fast," because the ball bounces "low" and players must rush to get it.

CLAY

Clay, considered "slower" than grass, is among the most popular surfaces. Many clay courts have been constructed with a type of composition dressing on the surface. This covering is primarily designed to speed the drying of the courts after a rain, though it also can add some color. Clay courts require daily maintenance, including frequent cleaning and replacement of the marking tapes that form the boundary lines. The ball slows more than on grass because of the contact with the rougher surface, and it bounces up higher, giving the player more time to return the shot.

CONCRETE AND ASPHALT

The primary advantage of these courts is very low required maintenance. Once the court is installed, only occasional brushing and repainting are needed. The surface is very fast, the ball bouncing higher than on grass or clay. A slight degree of coarseness on the surface is sometimes used to slow the ball. Concrete is hard on feet, shoes, and balls. "All weather" courts are very similar to concrete but have an added layer of asphalt composition on the surface. This surface provides some cushioning and helps with drainage. These so-called "hard courts" play very much like concrete.

SYNTHETICS

A number of artificial or synthetic court surfaces are also now available. These include carpetlike materials and types of plastics which are placed over a thin layer of foam. The play of these courts is much like that of grass, though there is a more consistent bounce. The courts are easy on the feet and do not require much maintenance. The speed can be altered depending upon the type of materials used. Many of these newer surfaces are being used both indoors and outdoors.

EQUIPMENT EXPENSE LOG

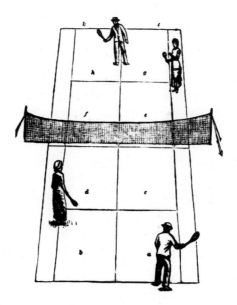

The Tennis Expense Log is designed to help you keep track of your tennis-related expenses, from racquets to equipment maintenance to court rentals to balls.

By recording the date of an expense or purchase, the location of the service or store, the individual items, their description and cost, you establish an ongoing record of expenses as well as a source directory for equipment, repairs, and service.

This log can also be used as an equipment quality checklist, reminding you of the location of the shop that offered particular bargains, or the name of the craftsman who so perfectly fitted your fine leather grip a year ago. Keep the log up to date in a methodical manner, and it will serve you for years to come.

DATE	SOURCE	ITEMS	COST
		TOTAL	

DATE	SOURCE	ITEMS	COST
			TOTAL

DATE	SOURCE	ITEMS	COST
		TOTAL	

DATE	SOURCE	ITEMS	COST
			TOTAL

DATE	SOURCE	ITEMS	COST
		TOTAL	

DATE	SOURCE	ITEMS	COST
		TOTAL	

DATE	SOURCE	ITEMS	COST
		TOTAL	

DATE	SOURCE	ITEMS	COST
		TOTAL	

DATE	SOURCE	ITEMS	COST
		TOTAL	

TENNIS DATES

Use the Tennis Dates Log as a schedule of your upcoming matches, lessons, clinics, and practice sessions.

The log provides space for the date of the event, where it is to take place, and the time. There is also space for listing the players or participants, and any comments or personal suggestions you have.

DATE	COURTS / LOCATION	TIME

PLAYERS / COMMENTS

DATE	COURTS / LOCATION	TIME

PLAYERS / COMMENTS

DATE	COURTS / LOCATION	TIME

PLAYERS / COMMENTS

DATE	COURTS / LOCATION	TIME

PLAYERS / COMMENTS

DATE	COURTS / LOCATION	TIME

PLAYERS / COMMENTS

DATE	COURTS / LOCATION	TIME

PLAYERS / COMMENTS

DATE	COURTS / LOCATION	TIME

PLAYERS / COMMENTS

DATE	COURTS / LOCATION	TIME

PLAYERS / COMMENTS

DATE	COURTS / LOCATION	TIME

PLAYERS / COMMENTS

DATE	COURTS / LOCATION	TIME

PLAYERS / COMMENTS

DATE	COURTS / LOCATION	TIME

PLAYERS / COMMENTS

DATE	COURTS / LOCATION	TIME

PLAYERS / COMMENTS

DATE	COURTS / LOCATION	TIME

PLAYERS / COMMENTS

DATE	COURTS / LOCATION	TIME

PLAYERS / COMMENTS

DATE	COURTS / LOCATION	TIME

PLAYERS / COMMENTS

DATE	COURTS / LOCATION	TIME

PLAYERS / COMMENTS

DATE	COURTS / LOCATION	TIME

PLAYERS / COMMENTS

DATE	COURTS / LOCATION	TIME

PLAYERS / COMMENTS

DATE	COURTS / LOCATION	TIME

PLAYERS / COMMENTS

DATE	COURTS / LOCATION	TIME

PLAYERS / COMMENTS

DATE	COURTS / LOCATION	TIME

PLAYERS / COMMENTS

DATE	COURTS / LOCATION	TIME

PLAYERS / COMMENTS

DATE	COURTS / LOCATION	TIME

PLAYERS / COMMENTS

DATE	COURTS / LOCATION	TIME

PLAYERS / COMMENTS

DATE	COURTS / LOCATION	TIME

PLAYERS / COMMENTS

DATE	COURTS / LOCATION	TIME

PLAYERS / COMMENTS

DATE	COURTS / LOCATION	TIME

PLAYERS / COMMENTS

DATE	COURTS / LOCATION	TIME

PLAYERS / COMMENTS

DATE	COURTS / LOCATION	TIME

PLAYERS / COMMENTS

DATE	COURTS / LOCATION	TIME

PLAYERS / COMMENTS

DATE	COURTS / LOCATION	TIME

PLAYERS / COMMENTS

DATE	COURTS / LOCATION	TIME

PLAYERS / COMMENTS

DATE	COURTS / LOCATION	TIME

PLAYERS / COMMENTS

DATE	COURTS / LOCATION	TIME

PLAYERS / COMMENTS

DATE	COURTS / LOCATION	TIME

PLAYERS / COMMENTS

DATE	COURTS / LOCATION	TIME

PLAYERS / COMMENTS

DATE	COURTS / LOCATION	TIME

PLAYERS / COMMENTS

DATE	COURTS / LOCATION	TIME

PLAYERS / COMMENTS

DATE	COURTS / LOCATION	TIME

PLAYERS / COMMENTS

DATE	COURTS / LOCATION	TIME

PLAYERS / COMMENTS

DATE	COURTS / LOCATION	TIME

PLAYERS / COMMENTS

DATE	COURTS / LOCATION	TIME

PLAYERS / COMMENTS

DATE	COURTS / LOCATION	TIME

PLAYERS / COMMENTS

DATE	COURTS / LOCATION	TIME

PLAYERS / COMMENTS

LESSON LOG

Good tennis requires agility, concentration, and coordination, and the development of the basic skills. For the latter you need a teacher.

Choosing a tennis pro, like selecting a tennis racquet, is a very personal decision. The rule of thumb remains the same: Do whatever seems the most comfortable to you. There are, however, some guidelines.

If you can't get any recommendations from friends or a club, contact your local community recreation department. Or try the tennis coach at the high school or a nearby college. Once you have a name it's a good idea to find out if the person belongs to the USPTA, which administers tests to all members. Finally, before signing up, watch the pro give a lesson. This is commonly done and neither you nor the pro should feel awkward. Once you've seen an instructor in action, you can determine whether the two of you will hit it off.

PATIENCE

Improving your game, especially if you're relatively new to tennis, can and will be tough. The most important thing is to be patient. Progress will come, but only with hard work. At first you may become frustrated. But remember that you're not alone. There are thousands of others going through just what you are experiencing – and thousands more who have succeeded and are enjoying playing better tennis. Finally, remember that the pro has a great deal of experience and knowledge. An instructor may tell you things that don't immediately make sense to you, or that may feel just plain wrong. He or she may, for example, suggest that you use a different grip, or position your body differently. That's the instructor's job – to teach you the proper way to execute the individual tennis strokes. And this may mean the unlearning of some bad habits. The teacher, though, should be encouraging at the same time. You need to feel confident in your teacher, as well as confident that with the proper amount of care and practice, your game will improve and you will enjoy tennis that much more.

PRACTICE

Practice. Over and over again. You'll never improve without practice. It's that simple. The difference between a good and an average tennis player is often the amount of practice. Watching good tennis or reading about it can help. But nothing can substitute for actually hitting the ball on the court.

The essence of practice is repetition. Repeat: The essence of practice is repetition. Practice is performing the same exercise over and over. That's precisely why so many avoid it. But it can also be exhilarating if you can tell you're improving and learning how to make your adjustments to your strokes on your own.

When practicing, concentrate on one stroke at a time. Think about what you have learned. Try carefully to stroke the ball, rather than slamming it. If you're with a partner, work on the weakest points of each other's games. Try serving while your partner practices service returns. Most important, be serious about your practice. Don't feel you have to beat your partner. You're not just playing to win, you're playing to improve. You should strike a medium between playing competitive sets and running through drills. And try practice matches. Develop games in which you use only certain ground strokes or where the focus is on how well you can complete a specific stroke.

Backboards are also helpful if they are used properly. Don't just slam the ball against the wall until you're tired. Instead, practice hitting the ball smoothly. On the court, try setting up targets (tennis cans will do) at the corner of the service box or near the baseline to improve the accuracy and depth of your shots. And save those old, worn balls. With a bucket of these, practice your serve out on the court when you don't have a partner to return them.

The Lesson Log is designed to help you get the most out of your lessons and practice sessions. Use the Lesson Log to record instructor's tips as well as your own thoughts after each lesson. They can be general notes, or specific corrections, such as a remedy for a particular problem with your forehand. If used as a reference, these records can help you ward off a tendency to revert to previous, often bad habits.

DATE TIME	INSTRUCTOR / LOCATION	SESSION LENGTH

SHOTS / DETAILS WORKED ON

RESULTS / POINTS TO REMEMBER

DATE TIME	INSTRUCTOR / LOCATION	SESSION LENGTH

SHOTS / DETAILS WORKED ON

RESULTS / POINTS TO REMEMBER

DATE TIME	INSTRUCTOR / LOCATION	SESSION LENGTH

SHOTS / DETAILS WORKED ON

RESULTS / POINTS TO REMEMBER

DATE TIME	INSTRUCTOR / LOCATION	SESSION LENGTH

SHOTS / DETAILS WORKED ON

RESULTS / POINTS TO REMEMBER

DATE TIME	INSTRUCTOR / LOCATION	SESSION LENGTH

SHOTS / DETAILS WORKED ON

RESULTS / POINTS TO REMEMBER

DATE TIME	INSTRUCTOR / LOCATION	SESSION LENGTH

SHOTS / DETAILS WORKED ON

RESULTS / POINTS TO REMEMBER

DATE TIME	INSTRUCTOR / LOCATION	SESSION LENGTH

SHOTS / DETAILS WORKED ON

RESULTS / POINTS TO REMEMBER

DATE TIME	INSTRUCTOR / LOCATION	SESSION LENGTH

SHOTS / DETAILS WORKED ON

RESULTS / POINTS TO REMEMBER

DATE TIME	INSTRUCTOR / LOCATION	SESSION LENGTH

SHOTS / DETAILS WORKED ON

RESULTS / POINTS TO REMEMBER

DATE TIME	INSTRUCTOR / LOCATION	SESSION LENGTH

SHOTS / DETAILS WORKED ON

RESULTS / POINTS TO REMEMBER

DATE TIME	INSTRUCTOR / LOCATION	SESSION LENGTH

SHOTS / DETAILS WORKED ON

RESULTS / POINTS TO REMEMBER

DATE TIME	INSTRUCTOR / LOCATION	SESSION LENGTH

SHOTS / DETAILS WORKED ON

RESULTS / POINTS TO REMEMBER

DATE TIME	INSTRUCTOR / LOCATION	SESSION LENGTH

SHOTS / DETAILS WORKED ON

RESULTS / POINTS TO REMEMBER

DATE TIME	INSTRUCTOR / LOCATION	SESSION LENGTH

SHOTS / DETAILS WORKED ON

RESULTS / POINTS TO REMEMBER

DATE TIME	INSTRUCTOR / LOCATION	SESSION LENGTH

SHOTS / DETAILS WORKED ON

RESULTS / POINTS TO REMEMBER

DATE TIME	INSTRUCTOR / LOCATION	SESSION LENGTH

SHOTS / DETAILS WORKED ON

RESULTS / POINTS TO REMEMBER

DATE TIME	INSTRUCTOR / LOCATION	SESSION LENGTH

SHOTS / DETAILS WORKED ON

RESULTS / POINTS TO REMEMBER

DATE TIME	INSTRUCTOR / LOCATION	SESSION LENGTH

SHOTS / DETAILS WORKED ON

RESULTS / POINTS TO REMEMBER

RULES
OF THE GAME

Though players bang the balls from one end of the court to the other and often grunt with each stroke, tennis is really quite a refined game. It has a special history, a special scoring system, and a special set of rules for regular play or competition. This includes a different set of rules that govern personal conduct on and off the court. They apply to the professional as well as to the beginner.

Your manner on the court is important. Some forms of behavior, such as cursing loudly, can be extremely distracting, not only to your opponent, but to others nearby. Your conduct projects an image that others can easily discern. It says a lot about the kind of player you actually are. And poor conduct is never appreciated.

There are some very basic rules of tennis etiquette. Control your temper and treat your opponent with courtesy and respect. This can even improve your game. Instead of yelling about the shot you missed, or blaming your grip, relax and think about your game and how you can improve it. Losing your temper will only tend to disturb your concentration (as well as that of others), and this can only make things worse.

You should dress appropriately. Today this means that you must wear the traditional all white at only a select few clubs (but it means wearing the proper tennis shoes everywhere). Some other guidelines to remember are:

■ When warming up before a match, take it easy. Don't start competing with your opponent until you begin keeping score.

■ When you're ready to begin serving, simply hold up the tennis balls so your opponent can see them and say, "Play these" or "These go." If you want to play "first one in," ask before you begin your serve.

■ The server should always keep score and should call it out periodically, especially at the beginning of each game, so that there are no misunderstandings.

■ If the ball lands on any part of the line, it is considered good. Whoever is in the best position to make the call should do so – this may mean that your opponent may make some calls on your side, especially on some down the line shots. If neither you nor your opponent can confidently make a call, assume it was good.

■ Immediately call a "let" and play the point over if a stray ball from a nearby court rolls onto yours.

■ Don't walk behind a nearby court until play has stopped. If one of your balls rolls into an adjoining court, politely ask the other player to help you out.

■ Let your opponent know if you think he or she has hit a "good shot."

THE RULES OF TENNIS

1–Dimensions and Equipment

The court shall be a rectangle 78 feet (23.77m) long and 27 feet (8.23m) wide. It shall be divided across the middle by a net suspended from a cord or metal cable of a maximum diameter of one-third of an inch (0.8cm), the ends of which shall be attached to, or pass over, the tops of two posts, 3 feet 6 inches (1.07m) high, and not more than 6 inches (15cm) in diameter, the centers of which shall be 3 feet (0.91m) outside the court on each side. The net shall be extended fully so that it fills completely the space between the two posts and shall be of sufficiently small mesh to prevent the ball's passing through. The height of the net shall be 3 feet (0.914m) at the center where it shall be held down taut by a strap not more than 2 inches (5cm) wide and white in color. There shall be a band covering the cord or metal cable and the top of the net for not less than 2 inches (5cm) nor more than 2½ inches (6.3cm) in depth on each side and white in color. There shall be no advertisement on the net, strap, band or singles sticks. The lines bounding the ends and sides of the Court shall respectively be called the Baselines and the Sidelines. On each side of the net, at a distance of 21 feet (6.40m) from it and parallel with it, shall be drawn the Service lines. The space on each side of the net between the service line and the sidelines shall be divided into two equal parts, called the service courts, by the center service line, which must be 2 inches (5cm) in width, drawn half-way between, and parallel with, the sidelines. Each baseline shall be bisected by an imaginary continuation of the center service line to a line 4 inches (10cm) in length and 2 inches (5cm) in width called the center mark, drawn inside the Court at right angles to and in contact with such baselines. All other lines shall be not less than 1 inch (2.5cm) nor

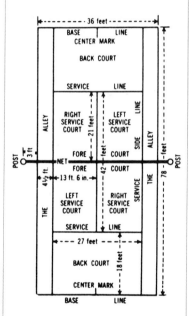

more than 2 inches (5cm) in width, except the baseline, which may be 4 inches (10cm) in width, and all measurements shall be made to the outside of the lines.

2–Permanent Fixtures

The permanent fixtures of the Court shall include not only the net, posts, cord or metal cable, strap and band, but also, where there are any such,

the back and side stops, the stands, fixed or movable seats and chairs around the Court, and their occupants, all other fixtures around and above the Court, and the Chair Umpire, Net Umpire, Line Umpires and Ball Boys when in their respective places.

3–Ball – Size. Weight and Bound

The ball shall have a uniform outer surface and shall be white or yellow in color. If there are any seams they shall be stitchless. The ball shall be more than two and a half inches (6.35cm) and less than two and five-eighths inches (6.67cm) in diameter, and more than two ounces (56.7 grams) and less than two and one-sixteenth ounces (58.5 grams) in weight. The ball shall have a bound of more than 53 inches (135cm) and less than 58 inches (147cm) when dropped 100 inches (254cm) upon a concrete base. The ball shall have a forward deformation of more than .220 of an inch (.56cm) and less than .290 of an inch (.74cm) and a return deformation of more than .350 of an inch (.89cm) and less than .425 of an inch (1.08cm) at 18 lbs. (8.165kg) load. The two deformation figures shall be the averages of three individual readings along three axes of the ball and no two individual readings shall differ by more than .030 of an inch (.08cm) in each case.

Regulations for conducting tests for bound, size and deformation of balls may be found in the USTA Yearbook or obtained from USTA in New York.

4–The Racket

The racket shall consist of a frame and a stringing. The frame may be of any material, weight, size or shape.

The strings must be alternately interlaced or bonded where they cross, and each string must be connected to the frame. If there are attachments, they must be used only to prevent wear and tear and must not alter the flight of the ball. The density in the center must be at least equal to the average density of the stringing. The stringing must be made so that the moves between the strings will not exceed that which is possible, for instance, with 18 mains and 18 crosses uniformly spaced and interlaced in a stringing area of 75 square inches.

5–Server and Receiver
The Player shall stand on opposite sides of the net; the player who first delivers the ball shall be called the Server, and the other the Receiver.

6–Choice of Ends and Service
The choice of ends and the right to be Server or Receiver in the first game shall be decided by toss. The player winning the toss may choose, or require his opponent to choose:
  a. The right to be Server or Receiver, in which case the other player shall choose the end; or
  b. The end, in which case the other player shall choose the right to be Server or Receiver.

7–Delivery of Service
The service shall be delivered in the following manner. Immediately before commencing to serve, the Server shall stand with both feet at rest behind (i.e. farther from the net than) the base-line, and within the imaginary continuations of the center-mark and side-line. The Server shall then project the ball by hand into the air in any direction and before it hits the ground strike it with his racket, and the delivery shall be deemed to have been completed at the moment of the impact of the racket and the ball. A player

with the use of only one arm may utilize his racket for the projection.

8–Foot Fault
The Server shall throughout the delivery of the service:
  a. Not change his position by walking or running.
  b. Not touch, with either foot, any area other than that behind the baseline within the imaginary extension of the center-mark and sideline.

9–From Alternate Courts
  a. In delivering the service, the Server shall stand alternately behind the right and left Courts, beginning from the right in every game. If service from a wrong half of the Court occurs and is undetected, all play resulting from such wrong service or services shall stand, but the inaccuracy of the station shall be corrected immediately it is discovered.
  b. The ball served shall pass over the net and hit the ground within the Service Court which is diagonally opposite, or upon any line bounding such Court, before the Receiver returns it.

10–Faults
The Service is a fault:
  a. If the Server commits any breach of Rules 7, 8 or 9;
  b. If he misses the ball in attempting to strike it;
  c. If the ball served touches a permanent fixture (other than the net, strap or band) before it hits the ground.

11–Service After a Fault
After a fault (if it be the first fault) the Server shall serve again from behind the same half of the Court

from which he served that fault, unless the service was from the wrong half, when, in accordance with Rule 9, the Server shall be entitled to one Service only from behind the other half. A fault may not be claimed after the next service has been delivered.

12-Receiver Must Be Ready
The Server shall not serve until the Receiver is ready. If the latter attempts to return the service, he shall be deemed ready. If, however, the Receiver signifies that he is not ready, he may not claim a fault because the ball does not hit the ground within the limits for the service.

13-A Let
In all cases where a let has to be called under the rules, or to provide for an interruption to play, it shall have the following interpretations:
  a. When called solely in respect of a service, that one service only shall be replayed.
  b. When called under any other circumstance, the point shall be replayed.

14-The Service Is A Let
The service is a let:
  a. If the ball served touches the net, strap or band, and is otherwise good, or, after touching the net, strap or band, touches the Receiver or anything which he wears or carries before hitting the ground.
  b. If a service or a fault is delivered when the Receiver is not ready (see Rule 12).
In case of a let, that particular service shall not count, and the Server shall serve again, but a service let does not annul a previous fault.

15-When Receiver Becomes Server
At the end of the first game the Receiver shall become the server, and the Server Receiver; and so on alternately in all the subsequent games of a match. If a player serves out of turn, the player who ought to have served shall serve as soon as the mistake is discovered, but all points scored before such discovery shall be reckoned. If a game shall have been completed before such discovery, the order of service remains as altered. A fault served before such discovery shall not be reckoned.

16-When Players Change Ends
The players shall change ends at the end of the first, third and every subsequent alternate game of each set, and at the end of each set unless the total number of games in such set be even, in which case the change is not made until the end of the first game of the next set.

If a mistake is made and the correct sequence is not followed the players must take up their correct station as soon as the discovery is made and follow their original sequence.

17-Ball in Play Till Point Decided
A ball is in play from the moment at which it is delivered in service. Unless a fault or let be called, it remains in play until the point is decided.

18-Server Wins Point
The Server wins the point:
  a. If the ball served, not being a let under Rule 14, touches the Receiver or anything which he wears or carries, before it hits the ground;
  b. If the Receiver otherwise loses the point as provided by Rule 20.

19–Receiver Wins Point

The Receiver wins the point:
a. If the Server serves two consecutive faults;
b. If the Server otherwise loses the point as provided by Rule 20.

20–Player Loses Point

A player loses the point if:
a. He fails, before the ball in play has hit the ground twice consecutively, to return it directly over the net (except as provided in Rule 24 (a) or (c)); or
b. He returns the ball in play so well it hits the ground, a permanent fixture, or other object, outside any of the lines which bound his opponent's Court (except as provided in Rule 24 (a) and (c)); or
c. He volleys the ball and fails to make a good return even when standing outside the Court; or
d. In playing the ball he deliberately carries or catches it on his racket or deliberately touches it with his racket more than once; or
e. He or his racket (in his hand or otherwise) or anything which he wears or carries touch the net, post (single stick, if they are in use), cord or metal cable, strap or band, or the ground within his opponent's Court at any time while the ball is in play (touching a pipe support running across the court at the bottom of the net is interpreted as touching the net); [See Note at Rule 23]; or
f. He volleys the ball before it has passed the net; or
g. The ball in play touches him or anything that he wears or carries, except his racket in his hand or hands; or
h. He throws his racket at and hits the ball.

21–Player Hinders Opponent

If a player commits any act which hinders his opponent in making a stroke, then, if this is deliberate, he shall lose the point or if involuntary, the point shall be replayed.

22–Ball Falling on Line – Good

A ball falling on a line is regarded as falling in the Court bounded by that line.

23–Ball Touching Permanent Fixture

If the ball in play touches a permanent fixture (other than the net, posts, cord or metal cable, strap or band) after it has hit the ground, the player who struck it wins the point; if before it hits the ground his opponent wins the point.

24–Good Return

It is a good return:
a. If the ball touches the net, post (singles stick, if they are in use), cord or metal cable, strap or band, provided that it passes over any of them and hits the ground within the Court; or
b. If the ball, served or returned, hits the ground within the proper Court and rebounds or is blown back over the net, and the player whose turn it is to strike reaches over the net and plays the ball, provided that neither he nor any part of his clothes or racket touch the net, post (single stick), cord or metal cable, strap or band or the ground within his opponent's Court, and that the stroke is otherwise good; or
c. If the ball is returned outside the post or singles stick, either above or below the level of the top of the net, even though it touches the post or singles stick, provided that it hits the ground within the proper Court; or
d. If a player's racket passes over the net after he has returned the

ball, provided the ball passes the net before being played and is properly returned; or

e. If a player succeeds in returning the ball, served or in play, which strikes a ball lying in the Court [i.e. on his court when the point started].

25–Interference

In case a player is hindered in making a stroke by anything not within his control except a permanent fixture of the Court, or except as provided for in Rule 21, the point shall be replayed.

26–The Game

If a player wins his first point, the score is called 15 for that player; on winning his second point, the score is called 30 for that player; on winning his third point, the score is called 40 for that player, and the fourth point won by a player is scored *game* for that player except as below:

If both players have won three points, the score is called *deuce;* and the next point won by a player is called *advantage* for that player. If the same player wins the next point, he wins the game; if the other player wins the next point the score is again called *deuce;* and so on until a player wins the two points immediately following the score at deuce, when the game is scored for that player.

27–The Set

A player (or players) who first wins six games wins a set; except that he must win by a margin of two games over his opponent and where necessary a set shall be extended until this margin be achieved.

28–Maximum Number of Sets

The maximum number of sets in a match shall be 5, or, where women take part, 3.

29–Rules Apply to Both Sexes

Except where otherwise stated, every reference in these Rules to the masculine includes the feminine gender.

30–Decisions of Umpire and Referee

In matches where a Chair Umpire is appointed his decision shall be final; but where a Referee is appointed an appeal shall lie to him from the decision of a Chair Umpire on a question of law, and in all such cases the decision of the Referee shall be final.

In matches where assistants to the Chair Umpire are appointed (Line Umpires, Net Umpire, Foot-fault Judge) their decisions shall be final on questions of fact, except that if, in the opinion of the Chair Umpire, a clear mistake has been made, he shall have the right to change the decision of an assistant or order a let to be played.

When such an assistant is unable to give a decision he shall indicate this immediately to the Chair Umpire who shall give a decision. When the Chair is unable to give a decision on a question of fact he shall order a let to be played.

In Davis Cup or other team matches where a Referee is on court, any decision can be changed by the Referee, who may also instruct the Chair Umpire to order a let to be played.

The Referee, in his discretion, may at any time postpone a match on account of darkness or the condition of the ground or the weather. In any case of postponement the previous score and previous occupancy of courts shall hold good, unless the Referee and the players unanimously agree otherwise.

31–Continuous Play
Play shall be continuous from the first service till the match is concluded:

a. Notwithstanding the above, after the third set, or when women take part the second set, either player is entitled to a rest, which shall not exceed 10 minutes, or, in countries situated between Latitude 15 degrees north and Latitude 15 degrees south, 45 minutes, and furthermore when necessitated by circumstances not within the control of the players the Chair Umpire may suspend play for such a period as he may consider necessary.

If play is suspended and not resumed until a day later, the rest may be taken only after the third set (or when women take part the second set) of play on such later day, completion of an unfinished set being counted as one set.

If play is suspended and not resumed until 10 minutes have elapsed in the same day, the rest may be taken only after three consecutive sets have been played without interruption (or when women take part two sets), completion of an unfinished set being counted as one set.

Any nation is at liberty to modify this provision or omit it from its regulations governing tournaments, matches or competitions held in its own country, other than the International Tennis Championships (Davis Cup and Federation Cup).

b. Play shall never be suspended, delayed or interfered with for the purpose of enabling a player to recover his strength or his breath.

c. A maximum of 30 seconds shall elapse from the end of one point to the time the ball is served for the next point, except that when changing ends a maximum of one minute 30 seconds shall elapse from the last point of one game to the time when the ball is served for the first point of the next game.

These provisions shall be strictly construed. The Chair Umpire shall be the sole judge of any suspension, delay or interference and after giving due warning he may disqualify the offender.

32–Coaching
During a match a player may not receive any coaching or advice, except that when a player changes ends he may receive instruction from a Captain who is sitting on the Court in a team competition.

33–Ball Change Error
In cases where balls are changed after an agreed number of games, if the balls are not changed in the correct sequence the mistake shall be corrected when the player, or pair in the case of doubles, who should have served with the new balls is next due to serve.

34–Dimensions of Court
For the Doubles Game the Court shall be 36 feet (10.97m) in width, i.e. 4½ feet (1.37m) wider on each side than the Court for the Singles Game, and those portions of the singles sidelines which lie between the two service lines shall be called the service sidelines. In other respects, the Court shall be similar to that described in Rule 1, but the portions of the singles sidelines between the baseline and the service line on each side of the next may be omitted if desired.

36–Order of Service
The order of serving shall be decided at the beginning of each set as follows:

The pair who have to serve in the first game of each set shall decide which partner shall do so and the opposing pair shall decide similarly for the second game. The partner of the player who served in the first game shall serve in the third; the partner of the player who served in the second game shall serve in the fourth, and so on in the same order in all subsequent games of a set.

37–Order of Receiving
The order of receiving the service shall be decided at the beginning of each set as follows:

The pair who have to receive the service in the first game shall decide which partner shall receive the first service, and that partner shall continue to receive the first service in every odd game, throughout the set. The opposing pair shall likewise decide which partner shall receive the first service in the second game and that partner shall continue to receive the first service in every even game throughout that set. Partners shall receive the service alternately throughout each game.

38–Service Out of Turn
If a partner serves out of his turn, the partner who ought to have served shall serve as soon as the mistake is discovered, but all points scored, and any faults served be-fore such discovery shall be reckoned. If a game shall have been completed before such discovery the order of service remains as altered.

39–Error in Order of Receiving
If during a game the order of receiving the service is changed by the receivers it shall remain as altered until the end of the game in which the mistake is discovered, but the partners shall resume their original order of receiving in the next game of that set in which they are receivers of the service.

40–Ball Touching Server's Partner Is Fault
The service is a fault as provided for by Rule 10, or if the ball served touches the Server's partner or anything which he wears or carries, not being a let under Rule 14 (a), before it hits the ground, the Server wins the point.

41–Ball Struck Alternately
The ball shall be struck alternately by one or other player of the opposing pairs, and if a player touches the ball in play with his racket in contravention of this Rule, his opponents win the point.

THE TWELVE-POINT TIE-BREAKER

The sudden-death tie-breaker is in effect any time a set reaches 6-all in games. Thus, no set can be longer than thirteen games. The twelve-point tie-breaker works as follows: **Singles.** When a set reaches 6-all Player A who would serve in normal rotation serves the first two points (right and left); B serves points 3 and 4 (right and left); A serves points 5 and 6 (right and left); the players change sides; Player B serves points 7 and 8; A serves 9 and 10; B serves 11 and 12. If either player wins 7 points, he wins the set 7 games to 6.

Upon completion of the tie-breaker game the player who served the last full game of the prior set serves the first game of the next set. After completion of that game the players change sides. If the tie-breaker game reaches 6 points all, the players change sides for 4 points and change every 4 points thereafter. The service shall alternate on every point. If either player establishes a margin of 2 points, the tie-breaker game and the set are concluded. In USTA-sanctioned tournaments, when the tie-breaker game reaches 6 points all, service is to alternate on every point until one player achieves a margin of 2 points and thereby wins the game and the set. The players or teams are to change sides at 6 points all and then after every 4 points (i.e., after points 12, 16, 20, etc.). No rest is permitted on these changes.

The ITF has sanctioned this form of tie-breaker for all major tournaments.

Doubles. The format for singles shall apply, and the service order shall continue during the tie-breaker game notwithstanding the circumstance that a player may serve in part from the end where he has not served during the body of the set.

In the 12-point game, it should be noted that service changes every 2 points and a change of sides occurs after the first 6 points of the tie-breaker game. This is in accordance with the procedure adopted by World Championship Tennis after consultation with the top professionals associated with that organization. WCT has announced it will invoke the tie-breaker at 5 games all, but USTA will adhere to the 6–6 level for the present, regardless of the tie-breaker system being used. The only complexity presented by the 7-out-of-12-point system arises in the occasional situation where the score reaches 6 points all.

VAN ALLEN SIMPLIFIED
SCORING SYSTEM

While all USTA rules apply except in scoring, there are two sets of VASSS rules as follows:

Rules of VASSS "No-Ad." This method permits accurate scheduling of tennis matches since the length of the game is fairly well controlled. It operates as follows:

1. The *advantage point* is eliminated in the game, and the *advantage game* in the set.

2. The first to win 4 points, 1-2-3-4 (not 15-30-40) wins the game, the first to win 6 games wins the set. However, where time is a factor, the set may be reduced from 6 to either 5 or 4 games. If the score is tied (5 games all) the 9-point tie-breaker decides the set. Maximum number of points 79, playing time 25 to 30 minutes.

Rules of VASSS "Single Point." This method offers an efficient way to handicap accurately and consists of the following:

1. Points are scored as in table tennis—1-2-3-4. . . .

2. The serve changes from A to B every 5 points (5, 10, 15, . . .). This 5-point sequence is called a "hand." Serve also changes at the end of the set.

3. The first point in each "hand" (1, 6, 11, 16, . . .) is served into the right, or forehand, court.

4. Sides are changed on the odd 5-point "hand" (5, 15, and 25).

5. The official set is fixed at 31 points. But where time is at a premium, 21 points may be used.

6. If there is no umpire the server is required to *call score loud and clear* after each point.

7. The winner of the set must lead by at least 2 points (31–29). Maximum number of points 69, playing time 25 to 30 minutes.

Nine-Point VASSS Tie-Breaker Rule. In the event the score is tied in "no-ad" at 5 games all or in "single point" at 30 points all, he who would normally serve the eleventh game in "no-ad" or the sixty-first point in "single point" shall serve points 1, 2, 5, 6, of the 5-out-of-9-point tie-breaker. Sides shall be changed after the first 4 points. The receiver in the tie-breaker game shall serve points 3 and 4, 7 and 8, and if the score shall reach 4 points all, he serves the ninth point into either the right or left court. Each player shall serve 2 points in succession, right-left, 1 and 2, 3 and 4, etc. At the end of the tie-breaker game the receiver in the first set (he who served points 3, 4, 7, 8, and 9 of the tie-breaker) shall commence serving in the second set. In the event the score is again tied in the second set, 5 games all, or 30 points all respectively, he shall serve points 1, 2, 5, and 6 of the tie-breaker game, etc., etc. If the sets are tied 1 set all in a 3-set match or 2 sets all in a 5-set match, the players shall spin the racket again for choice of service or side in the final set. The advantage enjoyed by Player B who serves the ninth point, providing the score is tied at 4–4, is offset by the fact that his opponent, Player A, serves 4 out of the first 6 points, namely, 1, 2, 5, and 6, and the fact that the ninth point may never be reached.

In doubles, the same player on team A serves points 1 and 2, his partner 5 and 6. On team B the same player serves points 3 and 4 and his partner points 7, 8, and 9. Each player shall serve from the side from which he served during the proceding games in the set.

In regular VASSS play, a match may be either 2 sets or 4 sets with the 9-point tie-breaker to decide the winner if sets are divided, or the regular 2 out of 3 or 3 out of 5 set match formula may be used.

THE NATIONAL TENNIS RATING PROGRAM

It is important to know how well you play tennis, relative to other players. For one thing, this knowledge serves as a guide to selecting partners and opponents for matches. Most prefer to play with others at or above their level of ability. Being able to judge and state your performance level accurately is also important if you are to discern any improvement.

Not surprisingly, many players find it difficult to rate their own abilities. Some underestimate themselves, more overestimate. Tennis pros can give you a good idea of your level of play. They can match you with others of roughly the same caliber and they can notice improvements in your game. But not all players regularly see a tennis pro, and many would prefer to work on their own. More important, players cannot all consult the same pro, so that comparing your abilities with those of others off the court has been virtually impossible.

With this in mind, tennis professionals have recently developed a simple program to enable tennis players to rate themselves. The National Tennis Rating Program was jointly introduced by three leading tennis organizations: the USTA, the United States Professional Tennis Association (representing teaching pros), and the National Tennis Association (representing club owners and operators).

The program is simple. You consult a table of thirteen brief classifications. Each describes in detail a generally recognized level of tennis play. These descriptions have been carefully prepared by tennis professionals and contain specific comments about each facet of the game.

The classifications are numbered from 1.0 to 7.0 (that is, 1.0, 1.5, 2.0, 2.5). You select the one that most accurately describes your level of play (above 5.5. is for top-level competitors). That number becomes your rating. If you have trouble deciding between two ratings, place yourself in the lower one. Naturally, your rating will change as you improve. It can easily be compared with those of other players throughout the country. The system was designed to replace such vague terms as "beginner" and "advanced." It provides the first common terminology for all players.

As the name implies, the self-rating program is for your benefit. It can help you single out opponents at a level most compatible with your game. It also provides a way to measure your progress as you compare your skills against those outlined in the descriptions. If you wish, the rating may also be verified by a teaching professional or other qualified expert.

1.0 – This player is just starting to play tennis.

1.5 – This player has played a limited amount but is still working primarily on getting the ball over the net; has some knowledge of scoring but is not familiar with basic positions and procedures for singles and doubles play.

2.0 – This player may have had some lessons but needs on-court experience; has obvious stroke weaknesses but is beginning to feel comfortable with singles and doubles play.

2.5 – This player has more dependable strokes but is still unable to judge where the ball is going; has weak court coverage; is still working just to keep the ball in play with others of the same ability.

3.0 – This player can place shots with moderate success; can sustain a rally of slow pace but is not comfortable with all strokes; lacks consistency in serving.

3.5 – This player still lacks stroke dependability, depth and variety but has improved ability to direct shots away from opponent; rarely double faults but does not usually force errors on the serve; hits forehand and backhand volleys with consistency if the ball is within reach.

4.0 – This player has dependable strokes on both forehand and backhand sides; has the ability to use a variety of shots including lobs, overheads, approach shots and volleys; can position in a doubles game.

4.5 – This player has begun to master the use of power and spins; has sound footwork; can control depth of shots and is able to move opponent up and back; can hit first serves with above average power and accuracy and place the second serve; is able to rush net with some success on serve against players of similar ability.

5.0 – This player has good shot anticipation; is able to overcome some stroke deficiencies with outstanding shots or exceptional consistency; will approach net at opportune times and is often able to force an error or make a winning placement; can execute lobs, drop shots, half-volleys and overhead smashes with above average success; is able to vary the spin on the serve.

5.5 – This player is able to execute all strokes offensively and defensively; can hit first serves for winners and second serves to set up an offensive situation; maintains a winning level of play in social tennis and can reach at least the quarter-finals or semi-finals of the highest level club or park championship.

6.0 – This player has mastered all of the above skills; is able to hit both slice and topspin serves; can vary strategies and styles of play in a competitive situation; is capable of being ranked in a major city or USTA district.

6.5 – This player has developed power and/or consistency as a major weapon; has all of the above skills as well as the concentration necessary for successful tournament play; is capable of earning a USTA sectional ranking.

7.0 – This player is highly skilled in all of the above categories; is a polished tournament player who has travelled extensively for sanctioned competitions; has been ranked nationally by the USTA.

THE MATCH LOG

The Match Log is designed so that you can record partners and opponents, the weather and court surface conditions, and the match results. There is also space for personal comments and for notations concerning tactics that work for you or against you, and the characteristically strong or weak points of your partners and opponents.

Perhaps the most important section of the log is the personal box score where you can analyze your play. Consider the different elements of your game (serves, forehands, backhands, and lobs, volleys, and drop-shots, etc.) and note whether your play is above (+), below (–), or at (0) your usual standard. Also rate yourself for consistency. On the basis of this, you can judge the quality of your play. Are you playing better (+), worse (–), or about the same (0) as usual?

A tennis player becomes a better tennis player through practice, playing the game, and self-analysis. You should be able to determine which points of your game need improvement and which you need to concentrate on during practice sessions.

DATE	PARTNER / OPPONENT		LOCATION	

WEATHER / SURFACE		SCORES	

COMMENTS

SELF-RATING

SERVES	FOREHAND	BACKHAND	LOBS, VOLLEYS, DROPS, etc.	CONSISTENCY	OVERALL

DATE	PARTNER / OPPONENT		LOCATION	

WEATHER / SURFACE		SCORES	

COMMENTS

SELF-RATING

SERVES	FOREHAND	BACKHAND	LOBS, VOLLEYS, DROPS, etc.	CONSISTENCY	OVERALL

DATE	PARTNER / OPPONENT	LOCATION

WEATHER / SURFACE	SCORES

COMMENTS

SELF-RATING

SERVES	FOREHAND	BACKHAND	LOBS, VOLLEYS, DROPS, etc.	CONSISTENCY	OVERALL

DATE	PARTNER / OPPONENT	LOCATION

WEATHER / SURFACE	SCORES

COMMENTS

SELF-RATING

SERVES	FOREHAND	BACKHAND	LOBS, VOLLEYS, DROPS, etc.	CONSISTENCY	OVERALL

DATE	PARTNER / OPPONENT	LOCATION

WEATHER / SURFACE	SCORES

COMMENTS

SELF-RATING

SERVES	FOREHAND	BACKHAND	LOBS, VOLLEYS, DROPS, etc.	CONSISTENCY	OVERALL

DATE	PARTNER / OPPONENT	LOCATION

WEATHER / SURFACE	SCORES

COMMENTS

SELF-RATING

SERVES	FOREHAND	BACKHAND	LOBS, VOLLEYS, DROPS, etc.	CONSISTENCY	OVERALL

DATE	PARTNER / OPPONENT			LOCATION	

WEATHER / SURFACE		SCORES	

COMMENTS

SELF-RATING

SERVES	FOREHAND	BACKHAND	LOBS, VOLLEYS, DROPS, etc.	CONSISTENCY	OVERALL

DATE	PARTNER / OPPONENT			LOCATION	

WEATHER / SURFACE		SCORES	

COMMENTS

SELF-RATING

SERVES	FOREHAND	BACKHAND	LOBS, VOLLEYS, DROPS, etc.	CONSISTENCY	OVERALL

DATE	PARTNER / OPPONENT	LOCATION

WEATHER / SURFACE	SCORES

COMMENTS

SELF-RATING

SERVES	FOREHAND	BACKHAND	LOBS, VOLLEYS, DROPS, etc.	CONSISTENCY	OVERALL

DATE	PARTNER / OPPONENT	LOCATION

WEATHER / SURFACE	SCORES

COMMENTS

SELF-RATING

SERVES	FOREHAND	BACKHAND	LOBS, VOLLEYS, DROPS, etc.	CONSISTENCY	OVERALL

DATE	PARTNER / OPPONENT	LOCATION

WEATHER / SURFACE	SCORES

COMMENTS

SELF-RATING

SERVES	FOREHAND	BACKHAND	LOBS, VOLLEYS, DROPS, etc.	CONSISTENCY	OVERALL

DATE	PARTNER / OPPONENT	LOCATION

WEATHER / SURFACE	SCORES

COMMENTS

SELF-RATING

SERVES	FOREHAND	BACKHAND	LOBS, VOLLEYS, DROPS, etc.	CONSISTENCY	OVERALL

DATE	PARTNER / OPPONENT	LOCATION

WEATHER / SURFACE	SCORES

COMMENTS

SELF-RATING

SERVES	FOREHAND	BACKHAND	LOBS, VOLLEYS, DROPS, etc.	CONSISTENCY	OVERALL

DATE	PARTNER / OPPONENT	LOCATION

WEATHER / SURFACE	SCORES

COMMENTS

SELF-RATING

SERVES	FOREHAND	BACKHAND	LOBS, VOLLEYS, DROPS, etc.	CONSISTENCY	OVERALL

DATE	PARTNER / OPPONENT	LOCATION

WEATHER / SURFACE	SCORES

COMMENTS

SELF-RATING

SERVES	FOREHAND	BACKHAND	LOBS, VOLLEYS, DROPS, etc.	CONSISTENCY	OVERALL

DATE	PARTNER / OPPONENT	LOCATION

WEATHER / SURFACE	SCORES

COMMENTS

SELF-RATING

SERVES	FOREHAND	BACKHAND	LOBS, VOLLEYS, DROPS, etc.	CONSISTENCY	OVERALL

DATE	PARTNER / OPPONENT	LOCATION

WEATHER / SURFACE	SCORES

COMMENTS

SELF-RATING

SERVES	FOREHAND	BACKHAND	LOBS, VOLLEYS, DROPS, etc.	CONSISTENCY	OVERALL

DATE	PARTNER / OPPONENT	LOCATION

WEATHER / SURFACE	SCORES

COMMENTS

SELF-RATING

SERVES	FOREHAND	BACKHAND	LOBS, VOLLEYS, DROPS, etc.	CONSISTENCY	OVERALL

DATE	PARTNER / OPPONENT	LOCATION

WEATHER / SURFACE	SCORES

COMMENTS

SELF-RATING

SERVES	FOREHAND	BACKHAND	LOBS, VOLLEYS, DROPS, etc.	CONSISTENCY	OVERALL

DATE	PARTNER / OPPONENT	LOCATION

WEATHER / SURFACE	SCORES

COMMENTS

SELF-RATING

SERVES	FOREHAND	BACKHAND	LOBS, VOLLEYS, DROPS, etc.	CONSISTENCY	OVERALL

DATE	PARTNER / OPPONENT	LOCATION

WEATHER / SURFACE		SCORES

COMMENTS

SELF-RATING

SERVES	FOREHAND	BACKHAND	LOBS, VOLLEYS, DROPS, etc.	CONSISTENCY	OVERALL

DATE	PARTNER / OPPONENT	LOCATION

WEATHER / SURFACE		SCORES

COMMENTS

SELF-RATING

SERVES	FOREHAND	BACKHAND	LOBS, VOLLEYS, DROPS, etc.	CONSISTENCY	OVERALL

DATE	PARTNER / OPPONENT	LOCATION

WEATHER / SURFACE	SCORES

COMMENTS

SELF-RATING

SERVES	FOREHAND	BACKHAND	LOBS, VOLLEYS, DROPS, etc.	CONSISTENCY	OVERALL

DATE	PARTNER / OPPONENT	LOCATION

WEATHER / SURFACE	SCORES

COMMENTS

SELF-RATING

SERVES	FOREHAND	BACKHAND	LOBS, VOLLEYS, DROPS, etc.	CONSISTENCY	OVERALL

DATE	PARTNER / OPPONENT		LOCATION	

WEATHER / SURFACE		SCORES	

COMMENTS

SELF-RATING

SERVES	FOREHAND	BACKHAND	LOBS, VOLLEYS, DROPS, etc.	CONSISTENCY	OVERALL

DATE	PARTNER / OPPONENT		LOCATION	

WEATHER / SURFACE		SCORES	

COMMENTS

SELF-RATING

SERVES	FOREHAND	BACKHAND	LOBS, VOLLEYS, DROPS, etc.	CONSISTENCY	OVERALL

DATE	PARTNER / OPPONENT		LOCATION

WEATHER / SURFACE		SCORES

COMMENTS

SELF-RATING

SERVES	FOREHAND	BACKHAND	LOBS, VOLLEYS, DROPS, etc.	CONSISTENCY	OVERALL

DATE	PARTNER / OPPONENT		LOCATION

WEATHER / SURFACE		SCORES

COMMENTS

SELF-RATING

SERVES	FOREHAND	BACKHAND	LOBS, VOLLEYS, DROPS, etc.	CONSISTENCY	OVERALL

DATE	PARTNER / OPPONENT	LOCATION

WEATHER / SURFACE	SCORES

COMMENTS

SELF-RATING

SERVES	FOREHAND	BACKHAND	LOBS, VOLLEYS, DROPS, etc.	CONSISTENCY	OVERALL

DATE	PARTNER / OPPONENT	LOCATION

WEATHER / SURFACE	SCORES

COMMENTS

SELF-RATING

SERVES	FOREHAND	BACKHAND	LOBS, VOLLEYS, DROPS, etc.	CONSISTENCY	OVERALL

DATE	PARTNER / OPPONENT	LOCATION

WEATHER / SURFACE	SCORES

COMMENTS

SELF-RATING

SERVES	FOREHAND	BACKHAND	LOBS, VOLLEYS, DROPS, etc.	CONSISTENCY	OVERALL

DATE	PARTNER / OPPONENT	LOCATION

WEATHER / SURFACE	SCORES

COMMENTS

SELF-RATING

SERVES	FOREHAND	BACKHAND	LOBS, VOLLEYS, DROPS, etc.	CONSISTENCY	OVERALL

DATE	PARTNER / OPPONENT	LOCATION

WEATHER / SURFACE	SCORES

COMMENTS

SELF-RATING

SERVES	FOREHAND	BACKHAND	LOBS, VOLLEYS, DROPS, etc.	CONSISTENCY	OVERALL

DATE	PARTNER / OPPONENT	LOCATION

WEATHER / SURFACE	SCORES

COMMENTS

SELF-RATING

SERVES	FOREHAND	BACKHAND	LOBS, VOLLEYS, DROPS, etc.	CONSISTENCY	OVERALL

DATE	PARTNER / OPPONENT		LOCATION	

WEATHER / SURFACE		SCORES	

COMMENTS

SELF-RATING

SERVES	FOREHAND	BACKHAND	LOBS, VOLLEYS, DROPS, etc.	CONSISTENCY	OVERALL

DATE	PARTNER / OPPONENT		LOCATION	

WEATHER / SURFACE		SCORES	

COMMENTS

SELF-RATING

SERVES	FOREHAND	BACKHAND	LOBS, VOLLEYS, DROPS, etc.	CONSISTENCY	OVERALL

DATE	PARTNER / OPPONENT		LOCATION

WEATHER / SURFACE		SCORES

COMMENTS

SELF-RATING

SERVES	FOREHAND	BACKHAND	LOBS, VOLLEYS, DROPS, etc.	CONSISTENCY	OVERALL

DATE	PARTNER / OPPONENT		LOCATION

WEATHER / SURFACE		SCORES

COMMENTS

SELF-RATING

SERVES	FOREHAND	BACKHAND	LOBS, VOLLEYS, DROPS, etc.	CONSISTENCY	OVERALL

DATE	PARTNER / OPPONENT	LOCATION

WEATHER / SURFACE	SCORES

COMMENTS

SELF-RATING

SERVES	FOREHAND	BACKHAND	LOBS, VOLLEYS, DROPS, etc.	CONSISTENCY	OVERALL

DATE	PARTNER / OPPONENT	LOCATION

WEATHER / SURFACE	SCORES

COMMENTS

SELF-RATING

SERVES	FOREHAND	BACKHAND	LOBS, VOLLEYS, DROPS, etc.	CONSISTENCY	OVERALL

DATE	PARTNER / OPPONENT		LOCATION	

WEATHER / SURFACE		SCORES	

COMMENTS

SELF-RATING

SERVES	FOREHAND	BACKHAND	LOBS, VOLLEYS, DROPS, etc.	CONSISTENCY	OVERALL

DATE	PARTNER / OPPONENT		LOCATION	

WEATHER / SURFACE		SCORES	

COMMENTS

SELF-RATING

SERVES	FOREHAND	BACKHAND	LOBS, VOLLEYS, DROPS, etc.	CONSISTENCY	OVERALL

DATE	PARTNER / OPPONENT	LOCATION

WEATHER / SURFACE	SCORES

COMMENTS

SELF-RATING

SERVES	FOREHAND	BACKHAND	LOBS, VOLLEYS, DROPS, etc.	CONSISTENCY	OVERALL

DATE	PARTNER / OPPONENT	LOCATION

WEATHER / SURFACE	SCORES

COMMENTS

SELF-RATING

SERVES	FOREHAND	BACKHAND	LOBS, VOLLEYS, DROPS, etc.	CONSISTENCY	OVERALL

DATE	PARTNER / OPPONENT	LOCATION

WEATHER / SURFACE	SCORES

COMMENTS

SELF-RATING					
SERVES	FOREHAND	BACKHAND	LOBS, VOLLEYS, DROPS, etc.	CONSISTENCY	OVERALL

DATE	PARTNER / OPPONENT	LOCATION

WEATHER / SURFACE	SCORES

COMMENTS

SELF-RATING					
SERVES	FOREHAND	BACKHAND	LOBS, VOLLEYS, DROPS, etc.	CONSISTENCY	OVERALL

DATE	PARTNER / OPPONENT	LOCATION

WEATHER / SURFACE	SCORES

COMMENTS

SELF-RATING

SERVES	FOREHAND	BACKHAND	LOBS, VOLLEYS, DROPS, etc.	CONSISTENCY	OVERALL

DATE	PARTNER / OPPONENT	LOCATION

WEATHER / SURFACE	SCORES

COMMENTS

SELF-RATING

SERVES	FOREHAND	BACKHAND	LOBS, VOLLEYS, DROPS, etc.	CONSISTENCY	OVERALL

DATE	PARTNER / OPPONENT		LOCATION

WEATHER / SURFACE		SCORES

COMMENTS

SELF-RATING

SERVES	FOREHAND	BACKHAND	LOBS, VOLLEYS, DROPS, etc.	CONSISTENCY	OVERALL

DATE	PARTNER / OPPONENT		LOCATION

WEATHER / SURFACE		SCORES

COMMENTS

SELF-RATING

SERVES	FOREHAND	BACKHAND	LOBS, VOLLEYS, DROPS, etc.	CONSISTENCY	OVERALL

DATE	PARTNER / OPPONENT	LOCATION

WEATHER / SURFACE	SCORES

COMMENTS

SELF-RATING

SERVES	FOREHAND	BACKHAND	LOBS, VOLLEYS, DROPS, etc.	CONSISTENCY	OVERALL

DATE	PARTNER / OPPONENT	LOCATION

WEATHER / SURFACE	SCORES

COMMENTS

SELF-RATING

SERVES	FOREHAND	BACKHAND	LOBS, VOLLEYS, DROPS, etc.	CONSISTENCY	OVERALL

DATE	PARTNER / OPPONENT	LOCATION

WEATHER / SURFACE	SCORES

COMMENTS

SELF-RATING

SERVES	FOREHAND	BACKHAND	LOBS, VOLLEYS, DROPS, etc.	CONSISTENCY	OVERALL

DATE	PARTNER / OPPONENT	LOCATION

WEATHER / SURFACE	SCORES

COMMENTS

SELF-RATING

SERVES	FOREHAND	BACKHAND	LOBS, VOLLEYS, DROPS, etc.	CONSISTENCY	OVERALL

DATE	PARTNER / OPPONENT	LOCATION

WEATHER / SURFACE	SCORES

COMMENTS

SELF-RATING

SERVES	FOREHAND	BACKHAND	LOBS, VOLLEYS, DROPS, etc.	CONSISTENCY	OVERALL

DATE	PARTNER / OPPONENT	LOCATION

WEATHER / SURFACE	SCORES

COMMENTS

SELF-RATING

SERVES	FORFHAND	BACKHAND	LOBS, VOLLEYS, DROPS, etc.	CONSISTENCY	OVERALL

DATE	PARTNER / OPPONENT	LOCATION

WEATHER / SURFACE	SCORES

COMMENTS

SELF-RATING

SERVES	FOREHAND	BACKHAND	LOBS, VOLLEYS, DROPS, etc.	CONSISTENCY	OVERALL

DATE	PARTNER / OPPONENT	LOCATION

WEATHER / SURFACE	SCORES

COMMENTS

SELF-RATING

SERVES	FOREHAND	BACKHAND	LOBS, VOLLEYS, DROPS, etc.	CONSISTENCY	OVERALL

DATE	PARTNER / OPPONENT		LOCATION

WEATHER / SURFACE		SCORES

COMMENTS

SELF-RATING

SERVES	FOREHAND	BACKHAND	LOBS, VOLLEYS, DROPS, etc.	CONSISTENCY	OVERALL

DATE	PARTNER / OPPONENT		LOCATION

WEATHER / SURFACE		SCORES

COMMENTS

SELF-RATING

SERVES	FOREHAND	BACKHAND	LOBS, VOLLEYS, DROPS, etc.	CONSISTENCY	OVERALL

DATE	PARTNER / OPPONENT	LOCATION

WEATHER / SURFACE	SCORES

COMMENTS

SELF-RATING

SERVES	FOREHAND	BACKHAND	LOBS, VOLLEYS, DROPS, etc.	CONSISTENCY	OVERALL

DATE	PARTNER / OPPONENT	LOCATION

WEATHER / SURFACE	SCORES

COMMENTS

SELF-RATING

SERVES	FOREHAND	BACKHAND	LOBS, VOLLEYS, DROPS, etc.	CONSISTENCY	OVERALL

DATE	PARTNER / OPPONENT	LOCATION

WEATHER / SURFACE	SCORES

COMMENTS

SELF-RATING

SERVES	FOREHAND	BACKHAND	LOBS, VOLLEYS, DROPS, etc.	CONSISTENCY	OVERALL

DATE	PARTNER / OPPONENT	LOCATION

WEATHER / SURFACE	SCORES

COMMENTS

SELF-RATING

SERVES	FOREHAND	BACKHAND	LOBS, VOLLEYS, DROPS, etc.	CONSISTENCY	OVERALL

DATE	PARTNER / OPPONENT	LOCATION

WEATHER / SURFACE	SCORES

COMMENTS

SELF-RATING

SERVES	FOREHAND	BACKHAND	LOBS, VOLLEYS, DROPS, etc.	CONSISTENCY	OVERALL

DATE	PARTNER / OPPONENT	LOCATION

WEATHER / SURFACE	SCORES

COMMENTS

SELF-RATING

SERVES	FOREHAND	BACKHAND	LOBS, VOLLEYS, DROPS, etc.	CONSISTENCY	OVERALL

DATE	PARTNER / OPPONENT	LOCATION

WEATHER / SURFACE	SCORES

COMMENTS

SELF-RATING

SERVES	FOREHAND	BACKHAND	LOBS, VOLLEYS, DROPS, etc.	CONSISTENCY	OVERALL

DATE	PARTNER / OPPONENT	LOCATION

WEATHER / SURFACE	SCORES

COMMENTS

SELF-RATING

SERVES	FOREHAND	BACKHAND	LOBS, VOLLEYS, DROPS, etc.	CONSISTENCY	OVERALL

DATE	PARTNER / OPPONENT		LOCATION
.			

WEATHER / SURFACE		SCORES

COMMENTS

| | | | | | |

SELF-RATING

SERVES	FOREHAND	BACKHAND	LOBS, VOLLEYS, DROPS, etc.	CONSISTENCY	OVERALL

DATE	PARTNER / OPPONENT		LOCATION

WEATHER / SURFACE		SCORES

COMMENTS

| | | | | | |

SELF-RATING

SERVES	FOREHAND	BACKHAND	LOBS, VOLLEYS, DROPS, etc.	CONSISTENCY	OVERALL

DATE	PARTNER / OPPONENT	LOCATION

WEATHER / SURFACE	SCORES

COMMENTS

SELF-RATING

SERVES	FOREHAND	BACKHAND	LOBS, VOLLEYS, DROPS, etc.	CONSISTENCY	OVERALL

DATE	PARTNER / OPPONENT	LOCATION

WEATHER / SURFACE	SCORES

COMMENTS

SELF-RATING

SERVES	FOREHAND	BACKHAND	LOBS, VOLLEYS, DROPS, etc.	CONSISTENCY	OVERALL

DATE	PARTNER / OPPONENT	LOCATION

WEATHER / SURFACE	SCORES

COMMENTS

SELF-RATING

SERVES	FOREHAND	BACKHAND	LOBS, VOLLEYS, DROPS, etc.	CONSISTENCY	OVERALL

DATE	PARTNER / OPPONENT	LOCATION

WEATHER / SURFACE	SCORES

COMMENTS

SELF-RATING

SERVES	FOREHAND	BACKHAND	LOBS, VOLLEYS, DROPS, etc.	CONSISTENCY	OVERALL

DATE	PARTNER / OPPONENT	LOCATION

WEATHER / SURFACE	SCORES

COMMENTS

SELF-RATING

SERVES	FOREHAND	BACKHAND	LOBS, VOLLEYS, DROPS, etc.	CONSISTENCY	OVERALL

DATE	PARTNER / OPPONENT	LOCATION

WEATHER / SURFACE	SCORES

COMMENTS

SELF-RATING

SERVES	FOREHAND	BACKHAND	LOBS, VOLLEYS, DROPS, etc.	CONSISTENCY	OVERALL

DATE	PARTNER / OPPONENT	LOCATION

WEATHER / SURFACE	SCORES

COMMENTS

SELF-RATING

SERVES	FOREHAND	BACKHAND	LOBS, VOLLEYS, DROPS, etc.	CONSISTENCY	OVERALL

DATE	PARTNER / OPPONENT	LOCATION

WEATHER / SURFACE	SCORES

COMMENTS

SELF-RATING

SERVES	FOREHAND	BACKHAND	LOBS, VOLLEYS, DROPS, etc.	CONSISTENCY	OVERALL

DATE	PARTNER / OPPONENT		LOCATION

WEATHER / SURFACE		SCORES

COMMENTS

SELF-RATING

SERVES	FOREHAND	BACKHAND	LOBS, VOLLEYS, DROPS, etc.	CONSISTENCY	OVERALL

DATE	PARTNER / OPPONENT		LOCATION

WEATHER / SURFACE		SCORES

COMMENTS

SELF-RATING

SERVES	FOREHAND	BACKHAND	LOBS, VOLLEYS, DROPS, etc.	CONSISTENCY	OVERALL

DATE	PARTNER / OPPONENT		LOCATION	

WEATHER / SURFACE		SCORES	

COMMENTS

SELF-RATING

SERVES	FOREHAND	BACKHAND	LOBS, VOLLEYS, DROPS, etc.	CONSISTENCY	OVERALL

DATE	PARTNER / OPPONENT		LOCATION	

WEATHER / SURFACE		SCORES	

COMMENTS

SELF-RATING

SERVES	FOREHAND	BACKHAND	LOBS, VOLLEYS, DROPS, etc.	CONSISTENCY	OVERALL

DATE	PARTNER / OPPONENT	LOCATION

WEATHER / SURFACE	SCORES

COMMENTS

SELF-RATING					
SERVES	FOREHAND	BACKHAND	LOBS, VOLLEYS, DROPS, etc.	CONSISTENCY	OVERALL

DATE	PARTNER / OPPONENT	LOCATION

WEATHER / SURFACE	SCORES

COMMENTS

SELF-RATING					
SERVES	FOREHAND	BACKHAND	LOBS, VOLLEYS, DROPS, etc.	CONSISTENCY	OVERALL

DATE	PARTNER / OPPONENT	LOCATION

WEATHER / SURFACE	SCORES

COMMENTS

SELF-RATING

SERVES	FOREHAND	BACKHAND	LOBS, VOLLEYS, DROPS, etc.	CONSISTENCY	OVERALL

DATE	PARTNER / OPPONENT	LOCATION

WEATHER / SURFACE	SCORES

COMMENTS

SELF-RATING

SERVES	FOREHAND	BACKHAND	LOBS, VOLLEYS, DROPS, etc.	CONSISTENCY	OVERALL

DATE	PARTNER / OPPONENT	LOCATION

WEATHER / SURFACE	SCORES

COMMENTS

SELF-RATING

SERVES	FOREHAND	BACKHAND	LOBS, VOLLEYS, DROPS, etc.	CONSISTENCY	OVERALL

DATE	PARTNER / OPPONENT	LOCATION

WEATHER / SURFACE	SCORES

COMMENTS

SELF-RATING

SERVES	FOREHAND	BACKHAND	LOBS, VOLLEYS, DROPS, etc.	CONSISTENCY	OVERALL

DATE	PARTNER / OPPONENT	LOCATION

WEATHER / SURFACE	SCORES

COMMENTS

SELF-RATING

SERVES	FOREHAND	BACKHAND	LOBS, VOLLEYS, DROPS, etc.	CONSISTENCY	OVERALL

DATE	PARTNER / OPPONENT	LOCATION

WEATHER / SURFACE	SCORES

COMMENTS

SELF-RATING

SERVES	FOREHAND	BACKHAND	LOBS, VOLLEYS, DROPS, etc.	CONSISTENCY	OVERALL

DATE	PARTNER / OPPONENT	LOCATION

WEATHER / SURFACE	SCORES

COMMENTS

SELF-RATING

SERVES	FOREHAND	BACKHAND	LOBS, VOLLEYS, DROPS, etc.	CONSISTENCY	OVERALL

DATE	PARTNER / OPPONENT	LOCATION

WEATHER / SURFACE	SCORES

COMMENTS

SELF-RATING

SERVES	FOREHAND	BACKHAND	LOBS, VOLLEYS, DROPS, etc.	CONSISTENCY	OVERALL

DATE	PARTNER / OPPONENT		LOCATION

WEATHER / SURFACE		SCORES

COMMENTS

SELF-RATING

SERVES	FOREHAND	BACKHAND	LOBS, VOLLEYS, DROPS, etc.	CONSISTENCY	OVERALL

DATE	PARTNER / OPPONENT		LOCATION

WEATHER / SURFACE		SCORES

COMMENTS

SELF-RATING

SERVES	FOREHAND	BACKHAND	LOBS, VOLLEYS, DROPS, etc.	CONSISTENCY	OVERALL

DATE	PARTNER / OPPONENT	LOCATION

WEATHER / SURFACE	SCORES

COMMENTS

SELF-RATING

SERVES	FOREHAND	BACKHAND	LOBS, VOLLEYS, DROPS, etc.	CONSISTENCY	OVERALL

DATE	PARTNER / OPPONENT	LOCATION

WEATHER / SURFACE	SCORES

COMMENTS

SELF-RATING

SERVES	FOREHAND	BACKHAND	LOBS, VOLLEYS, DROPS, etc.	CONSISTENCY	OVERALL

DATE	PARTNER / OPPONENT		LOCATION

WEATHER / SURFACE		SCORES

COMMENTS

SELF-RATING

SERVES	FOREHAND	BACKHAND	LOBS, VOLLEYS, DROPS, etc.	CONSISTENCY	OVERALL

DATE	PARTNER / OPPONENT		LOCATION

WEATHER / SURFACE		SCORES

COMMENTS

SELF-RATING

SERVES	FOREHAND	BACKHAND	LOBS, VOLLEYS, DROPS, etc.	CONSISTENCY	OVERALL

DATE	PARTNER / OPPONENT	LOCATION

WEATHER / SURFACE	SCORES

COMMENTS

SELF-RATING

SERVES	FOREHAND	BACKHAND	LOBS, VOLLEYS, DROPS, etc.	CONSISTENCY	OVERALL

DATE	PARTNER / OPPONENT	LOCATION

WEATHER / SURFACE	SCORES

COMMENTS

SELF-RATING

SERVES	FOREHAND	BACKHAND	LOBS, VOLLEYS, DROPS, etc.	CONSISTENCY	OVERALL

DATE	PARTNER / OPPONENT		LOCATION	

WEATHER / SURFACE		SCORES	

COMMENTS

SELF-RATING

SERVES	FOREHAND	BACKHAND	LOBS, VOLLEYS, DROPS, etc.	CONSISTENCY	OVERALL

DATE	PARTNER / OPPONENT		LOCATION	

WEATHER / SURFACE		SCORES	

COMMENTS

SELF-RATING

SERVES	FOREHAND	BACKHAND	LOBS, VOLLEYS, DROPS, etc.	CONSISTENCY	OVERALL

DATE	PARTNER / OPPONENT	LOCATION

WEATHER / SURFACE	SCORES

COMMENTS

SELF-RATING					
SERVES	FOREHAND	BACKHAND	LOBS, VOLLEYS, DROPS, etc.	CONSISTENCY	OVERALL

DATE	PARTNER / OPPONENT	LOCATION

WEATHER / SURFACE	SCORES

COMMENTS

SELF-RATING					
SERVES	FOREHAND	BACKHAND	LOBS, VOLLEYS, DROPS, etc.	CONSISTENCY	OVERALL

DATE	PARTNER / OPPONENT	LOCATION

WEATHER / SURFACE	SCORES

COMMENTS

SELF-RATING

SERVES	FOREHAND	BACKHAND	LOBS, VOLLEYS, DROPS, etc.	CONSISTENCY	OVERALL

DATE	PARTNER / OPPONENT	LOCATION

WEATHER / SURFACE	SCORES

COMMENTS

SELF-RATING

SERVES	FOREHAND	BACKHAND	LOBS, VOLLEYS, DROPS, etc.	CONSISTENCY	OVERALL

DATE	PARTNER / OPPONENT	LOCATION

WEATHER / SURFACE	SCORES

COMMENTS

SELF-RATING

SERVES	FOREHAND	BACKHAND	LOBS, VOLLEYS, DROPS, etc.	CONSISTENCY	OVERALL

DATE	PARTNER / OPPONENT	LOCATION

WEATHER / SURFACE	SCORES

COMMENTS

SELF-RATING

SERVES	FOREHAND	BACKHAND	LOBS, VOLLEYS, DROPS, etc.	CONSISTENCY	OVERALL

DATE	PARTNER / OPPONENT	LOCATION

WEATHER / SURFACE		SCORES

COMMENTS

SELF-RATING

SERVES	FOREHAND	BACKHAND	LOBS, VOLLEYS, DROPS, etc.	CONSISTENCY	OVERALL

DATE	PARTNER / OPPONENT	LOCATION

WEATHER / SURFACE		SCORES

COMMENTS

SELF-RATING

SERVES	FOREHAND	BACKHAND	LOBS, VOLLEYS, DROPS, etc.	CONSISTENCY	OVERALL

TOURNAMENT LOG

Use this log to record your individual tournament play: how you fared, what worked, and what didn't.

The individual records include space for up to a 64-player draw. If the tournament or competition has 32, 16, or 8 players, simply enter your first round on the indicated line. For example, in a 16-player draw, record the results of your first round of play on the "Round of 16" line. If you receive a bye in the initial round, enter that, then begin recording your actual matches on the lines following. Use the space at the bottom to record the results of the tournament overall (i.e. the finalists, if you are not among them), the consolation matches, or your general comments.

ROUND	OPPONENT(S) / DATE	SCORES
ROUND of 64		
ROUND of 32		
ROUND of 16		
QUARTER-FINAL		
SEMI-FINAL		
FINAL		

TOURNAMENT: **DATES:**

SPONSOR / CLUB **PARTNER:**

SEMI-FINALS   FINAL   WINNER

SCORE:-

SCORE:-

SCORE:-

TOURNAMENT:		DATES:

SPONSOR / CLUB	PARTNER:

ROUND	OPPONENT(S) / DATE	SCORES
ROUND of 64		
ROUND of 32		
ROUND of 16		
QUARTER-FINAL		
SEMI-FINAL		
FINAL		

SEMI-FINALS	FINAL	WINNER

SCORE:———————

SCORE:———————

SCORE:———————

TOURNAMENT:			DATES:

SPONSOR / CLUB	PARTNER:

ROUND	OPPONENT(S) / DATE	SCORES
ROUND of 64		
ROUND of 32		
ROUND of 16		
QUARTER-FINAL		
SEMI-FINAL		
FINAL		

SEMI-FINALS   FINAL   WINNER

SCORE:——————————

SCORE:——————————

SCORE:——————————

ROUND	OPPONENT(S) / DATE	SCORES
ROUND of 64		
ROUND of 32		
ROUND of 16		
QUARTER-FINAL		
SEMI-FINAL		
FINAL		

TOURNAMENT:

DATES:

SPONSOR / CLUB

PARTNER:

SEMI-FINALS   FINAL   WINNER

SCORE:—————

SCORE:—————

SCORE:—————

ROUND	OPPONENT(S) / DATE	SCORES
ROUND of 64		
ROUND of 32		
ROUND of 16		
QUARTER-FINAL		
SEMI-FINAL		
FINAL		

TOURNAMENT:

DATES:

SPONSOR / CLUB

PARTNER:

SEMI-FINALS   FINAL   WINNER

SCORE:—

SCORE:—

SCORE:—

TOURNAMENT:		DATES:

SPONSOR / CLUB	PARTNER:

ROUND	OPPONENT(S) / DATE	SCORES
ROUND of 64		
ROUND of 32		
ROUND of 16		
QUARTER-FINAL		
SEMI-FINAL		
FINAL		

SEMI-FINALS   FINAL   WINNER

SCORE:————————

SCORE:————————

SCORE:————————

TOURNAMENT:		DATES:
SPONSOR / CLUB	PARTNER:	

ROUND	OPPONENT(S) / DATE	SCORES
ROUND of 64		
ROUND of 32		
ROUND of 16		
QUARTER-FINAL		
SEMI-FINAL		
FINAL		

SEMI-FINALS   FINAL   WINNER

SCORE:————

SCORE:————

SCORE:————

ROUND	OPPONENT(S) / DATE	SCORES
ROUND of 64		
ROUND of 32		
ROUND of 16		
QUARTER-FINAL		
SEMI-FINAL		
FINAL		

TOURNAMENT:

DATES:

SPONSOR / CLUB

PARTNER:

SEMI-FINALS　　　　　　　FINAL　　　　　　　WINNER

SCORE:———————

SCORE:———————

SCORE:———————

TOURNAMENT:		DATES:

SPONSOR / CLUB	PARTNER:

ROUND	OPPONENT(S) / DATE	SCORES
ROUND of 64		
ROUND of 32		
ROUND of 16		
QUARTER-FINAL		
SEMI-FINAL		
FINAL		

SEMI-FINALS	FINAL	WINNER

SCORE:——————

SCORE:——————

SCORE:——————

ROUND	OPPONENT(S) / DATE	SCORES
ROUND of 64		
ROUND of 32		
ROUND of 16		
QUARTER-FINAL		
SEMI-FINAL		
FINAL		

TOURNAMENT:

DATES:

SPONSOR / CLUB

PARTNER:

SEMI-FINALS   FINAL   WINNER

SCORE:―――――――

SCORE:―――――――

SCORE:―――――――

TOURNAMENT:		DATES:

SPONSOR / CLUB	PARTNER:

ROUND	OPPONENT(S) / DATE	SCORES
ROUND of 64		
ROUND of 32		
ROUND of 16		
QUARTER-FINAL		
SEMI-FINAL		
FINAL		

SEMI-FINALS	FINAL	WINNER

SCORE:———

SCORE:———

SCORE:———

TOURNAMENT:		DATES:

SPONSOR / CLUB	PARTNER:

ROUND	OPPONENT(S) / DATE	SCORES
ROUND of 64		
ROUND of 32		
ROUND of 16		
QUARTER-FINAL		
SEMI-FINAL		
FINAL		

SEMI-FINALS	FINAL	WINNER

SCORE:————————

SCORE:————————

SCORE:————————

TOURNAMENT:			DATES:

SPONSOR / CLUB	PARTNER:

ROUND	OPPONENT(S) / DATE	SCORES
ROUND of 64		
ROUND of 32		
ROUND of 16		
QUARTER-FINAL		
SEMI-FINAL		
FINAL		

SEMI-FINALS   FINAL   WINNER

SCORE:————————

SCORE:————————

SCORE:————————

138 TENNIS NOTES

TOURNAMENT:		DATES:

SPONSOR / CLUB	PARTNER:

ROUND	OPPONENT(S) / DATE	SCORES
ROUND of 64		
ROUND of 32		
ROUND of 16		
QUARTER-FINAL		
SEMI-FINAL		
FINAL		

SEMI-FINALS   FINAL   WINNER

SCORE:————

SCORE:————

SCORE:————

TOURNAMENT:			DATES:

SPONSOR / CLUB		PARTNER:

ROUND	OPPONENT(S) / DATE	SCORES
ROUND of 64		
ROUND of 32		
ROUND of 16		
QUARTER-FINAL		
SEMI-FINAL		
FINAL		

SEMI-FINALS   FINAL   WINNER

SCORE:—————————

SCORE:—————————

SCORE:—————————

NAMES & NUMBERS

The Names and Numbers Log is designed to become your source list of playing partners, equipment shops, instructors, clubs and courts, and anyone else who can provide you with information, assistance, and advice concerning your game.

INDIVIDUALS / ORGANIZATIONS	TELEPHONE
NAME:	
ADDRESS:	

COMMENTS / NOTES

INDIVIDUALS / ORGANIZATIONS	TELEPHONE
NAME:	
ADDRESS:	

COMMENTS / NOTES

INDIVIDUALS / ORGANIZATIONS	TELEPHONE
NAME:	
ADDRESS:	

COMMENTS / NOTES

INDIVIDUALS / ORGANIZATIONS	TELEPHONE
NAME:	
ADDRESS:	

COMMENTS / NOTES

INDIVIDUALS / ORGANIZATIONS	TELEPHONE
NAME:	
ADDRESS:	

COMMENTS / NOTES

INDIVIDUALS / ORGANIZATIONS	TELEPHONE
NAME:	
ADDRESS:	

COMMENTS / NOTES

INDIVIDUALS / ORGANIZATIONS	TELEPHONE
NAME:	
ADDRESS:	

COMMENTS / NOTES

INDIVIDUALS / ORGANIZATIONS	TELEPHONE
NAME:	
ADDRESS:	

COMMENTS / NOTES

INDIVIDUALS / ORGANIZATIONS	TELEPHONE
NAME:	
ADDRESS:	

COMMENTS / NOTES

INDIVIDUALS / ORGANIZATIONS	TELEPHONE
NAME:	
ADDRESS:	

COMMENTS / NOTES

INDIVIDUALS / ORGANIZATIONS	TELEPHONE
NAME:	
ADDRESS:	

COMMENTS / NOTES

INDIVIDUALS / ORGANIZATIONS	TELEPHONE
NAME:	
ADDRESS:	

COMMENTS / NOTES

INDIVIDUALS / ORGANIZATIONS	TELEPHONE
NAME:	
ADDRESS:	

COMMENTS / NOTES

INDIVIDUALS / ORGANIZATIONS	TELEPHONE
NAME:	
ADDRESS:	

COMMENTS / NOTES

INDIVIDUALS / ORGANIZATIONS	TELEPHONE
NAME:	
ADDRESS:	

COMMENTS / NOTES

INDIVIDUALS / ORGANIZATIONS	TELEPHONE
NAME:	
ADDRESS:	
COMMENTS / NOTES	

INDIVIDUALS / ORGANIZATIONS	TELEPHONE
NAME:	
ADDRESS:	
COMMENTS / NOTES	

INDIVIDUALS / ORGANIZATIONS	TELEPHONE
NAME:	
ADDRESS:	
COMMENTS / NOTES	

INDIVIDUALS / ORGANIZATIONS	TELEPHONE
NAME:	
ADDRESS:	

COMMENTS / NOTES

INDIVIDUALS / ORGANIZATIONS	TELEPHONE
NAME:	
ADDRESS:	

COMMENTS / NOTES

INDIVIDUALS / ORGANIZATIONS	TELEPHONE
NAME:	
ADDRESS:	

COMMENTS / NOTES

INDIVIDUALS / ORGANIZATIONS	TELEPHONE
NAME:	
ADDRESS:	

COMMENTS / NOTES

INDIVIDUALS / ORGANIZATIONS	TELEPHONE
NAME:	
ADDRESS:	

COMMENTS / NOTES

INDIVIDUALS / ORGANIZATIONS	TELEPHONE
NAME:	
ADDRESS:	

COMMENTS / NOTES

INDIVIDUALS / ORGANIZATIONS	TELEPHONE
NAME:	
ADDRESS:	

COMMENTS / NOTES

INDIVIDUALS / ORGANIZATIONS	TELEPHONE
NAME:	
ADDRESS:	

COMMENTS / NOTES

INDIVIDUALS / ORGANIZATIONS	TELEPHONE
NAME:	
ADDRESS:	

COMMENTS / NOTES

INDIVIDUALS / ORGANIZATIONS	TELEPHONE
NAME:	
ADDRESS:	

COMMENTS / NOTES

INDIVIDUALS / ORGANIZATIONS	TELEPHONE
NAME:	
ADDRESS:	

COMMENTS / NOTES

INDIVIDUALS / ORGANIZATIONS	TELEPHONE
NAME:	
ADDRESS:	

COMMENTS / NOTES

INDIVIDUALS / ORGANIZATIONS	TELEPHONE
NAME:	
ADDRESS:	

COMMENTS / NOTES

INDIVIDUALS / ORGANIZATIONS	TELEPHONE
NAME:	
ADDRESS:	

COMMENTS / NOTES

INDIVIDUALS / ORGANIZATIONS	TELEPHONE
NAME:	
ADDRESS:	

COMMENTS / NOTES

INDIVIDUALS / ORGANIZATIONS	TELEPHONE
NAME:	
ADDRESS:	

COMMENTS / NOTES

INDIVIDUALS / ORGANIZATIONS	TELEPHONE
NAME:	
ADDRESS:	

COMMENTS / NOTES

INDIVIDUALS / ORGANIZATIONS	TELEPHONE
NAME:	
ADDRESS:	

COMMENTS / NOTES

INDIVIDUALS / ORGANIZATIONS	TELEPHONE
NAME:	
ADDRESS:	

COMMENTS / NOTES

INDIVIDUALS / ORGANIZATIONS	TELEPHONE
NAME:	
ADDRESS:	

COMMENTS / NOTES

INDIVIDUALS / ORGANIZATIONS	TELEPHONE
NAME:	
ADDRESS:	

COMMENTS / NOTES

INDIVIDUALS / ORGANIZATIONS	TELEPHONE
NAME:	
ADDRESS:	

COMMENTS / NOTES

INDIVIDUALS / ORGANIZATIONS	TELEPHONE
NAME:	
ADDRESS:	

COMMENTS / NOTES

INDIVIDUALS / ORGANIZATIONS	TELEPHONE
NAME:	
ADDRESS:	

COMMENTS / NOTES

INDIVIDUALS / ORGANIZATIONS	TELEPHONE
NAME:	
ADDRESS:	

COMMENTS / NOTES

INDIVIDUALS / ORGANIZATIONS	TELEPHONE
NAME:	
ADDRESS:	

COMMENTS / NOTES

INDIVIDUALS / ORGANIZATIONS	TELEPHONE
NAME:	
ADDRESS:	

COMMENTS / NOTES

INDIVIDUALS / ORGANIZATIONS	TELEPHONE
NAME:	
ADDRESS:	

COMMENTS / NOTES

INDIVIDUALS / ORGANIZATIONS	TELEPHONE
NAME:	
ADDRESS:	

COMMENTS / NOTES

INDIVIDUALS / ORGANIZATIONS	TELEPHONE
NAME:	
ADDRESS:	

COMMENTS / NOTES

INDIVIDUALS / ORGANIZATIONS	TELEPHONE
NAME:	
ADDRESS:	

COMMENTS / NOTES

INDIVIDUALS / ORGANIZATIONS	TELEPHONE
NAME:	
ADDRESS:	

COMMENTS / NOTES

INDIVIDUALS / ORGANIZATIONS	TELEPHONE
NAME:	
ADDRESS:	

COMMENTS / NOTES

SELECTED READING

Anthony, Julie and Bollettieri, Nick. *A Winning Combination.* Scribner, 1980.

Ashe, Arthur. *Getting Started in Tennis.* Robinson, Louie, ed. Atheneum, 1979.

Ashe, Arthur, et al. *Mastering Your Tennis Strokes.* Sheehan, Larry, ed. Atheneum, 1976.

Barnaby, Jack. *Advantage Tennis: Racket Work, Tactics & Logic.* Allyn, 1975.

Barnaby, Jack. *Ground Strokes in Match Play.* Doubleday, 1978.

Beckett Howorth Dr., and Bender, Fred. *A Doctor's Answer to Tennis Elbow: How to Cure it, How to Prevent it.* Chelsea Hse. Pub., 1977.

Benjamin, David. *Competitive Tennis: A Parent's & Young Player's Guide.* Lippincott, 1979.

Borg, Bjorn and Scott, Eugene. *My Life and Game.* Simon & Schuster, 1980.

Bright, James, L. *The Tennis Court Book: A Player's Guide to Home Tennis Courts.* Brick Hse Pub., 1979.

Chilton's Editorial Staff. *Winning Tennis: Strokes & Strategy of the World's Top Pros Analysed by Dick Stockton & Wendy Overton.* Gillen, Bob, ed. Chilton, 1978.

Collins, Ed. *Watch the Ball, Bend Your Knees, That'll Be 20 Dollars Please.* Green Hill, 1977.

Duggan, Moira. *The Tennis Catalogue.* Macmillan, 1978.

Fiott, Steve. *Tennis Equipment.* Chilton, 1978.

Fox, Allan, and Evans, Richard. *If I'm the Better Player, Why Can't I win?* Tennis Mag., 1979.

Friedman, Sandra C. & Love Set, Inc. Staff, eds. *Tennis Lover's Year Round Travel Guide: A Complete Guide to Tennis Camps, Clinics & Resorts in the US, with Special Listings for the Carribean & Europe.* Acropolis.

Gallwey, W. Timothy. *The Inner Game of Tennis.* Bantam, 1979.

Harman, Bob and Monroe, Keith. *Use Your Head in Tennis.* Scribner, 1976.

Haynes, Connie. Kraft, Eve and Conroy, John. *Speed, Strength and Stamina: Conditioning for Tennis.* Doubleday, 1975.

Haynes, Connie & Kraft, Steven. *The Tennis Player's Diet: A Guide to Better Nutrition, on & off the Court.* Doubleday, 1978.

Hopman, Harry. *Better Tennis for Boys and Girls.* Dodd, 1972.

Hull, Gordon. *The Six Insidious Traps of College Tennis and How To Avoid Them.* Goodworth Pub., 1979.

Hunt, Leslie. *Inside Tennis for Women.* Contemporary Bks., 1978.

Johnson, Joan & Xanthos, Paul. *Tennis.* 3rd ed. William C. Brown, 1976.

Kraft, Steven, ed. *Tennis Drills for Self-Improvement.* Doubleday, 1978.

Kramer, Jack. *The Game—My Forty Years in Tennis.* Putnam, 1979.

Lowe, Jack. *Winning with Percentage Tennis.* Wilshire, 1977.

MacCurdy, Doug & Tully, Shawn. *Sports Illustrated Tennis.* Harper & Row, 1980.

Mason, Elaine. *Tennis.* Allyn, 1974.

Montgomery, Dr. Jim. *Tennis for the Mature Adult.* Hunter's Mountain Tennis Corp. 1980.

Morton, Jason. *Winning Tennis After Forty.* Prentice-Hall, 1980.

Murphy, Bill & Murphy, Chet. *Lifetime Treasury of Tested Tennis Tips: Secrets of Winning Play.* Prentice-Hall, 1978.

Neal, Charles, D. *Build Your Own Tennis Court: Constructing, Subcontracting, Equipping, and Maintaining Indoor and Outdoor Courts.* Chilton, 1978.

Rosewall, Ken. *Ken Rosewall on Tennis.* Fell, 1978.

Rosewall, Ken. *Play Tennis With Rosewall.* Wilshire, 1975.

Schickel, Richard. *The World of Tennis.* Random Hse, 1975.

Smith, Stan, et al. *Modern Tennis Doubles.* Sheehan, Larry, ed. Athenum, 1977.

Smith, Stan & Lutz, Bob. *Modern Tennis Doubles.* Atheneum, 1975.

Talbert, William F. and Old, Bruce, S. *The Game of Singles in Tennis.* Harper & Row, 1977.

Talbert, William F. and Old, Bruce, S. *The Game of Doubles in Tennis.* Harper & Row, 1977.

Talbert, Bill & Sports Illustrated Editors. *Sports Illustrated Tennis,* rev. ed. Lippincott, 1972.

Tarshis, Barry. *Tennis & the Mind.* Atheneum, 1977.

Tennis Magazine, eds. *The Tennis Player Handbook.* Simon & Schuster, 1980.

Tennis Magazine Editors, ed. *Tennis Strokes & Strategies.* (Fireside) Simon & Schuster, 1978.

Tilden, William T. *Match Play and the Spin of the Ball.* Arno.

Tilmanis, Gundars A. *Advanced Tennis for Coaches, Teachers and Players.* Lea & Febiger, 1975.

Tinling, Ted & Humphries, Rod. *Love & Faults.* Crown, 1979.

USTA Official Encyclopedia of Tennis. Harper & Row, 1979.

Wind, Herbert W. *Game, Set & Match: Great Moments in Tennis.* Dutton, 1979.

Wolff, Craig. *Tennis Superstars: The Men, Vol. 1.* Grosset & Dunlap, 1979.

The USTA Education & Research Center publishes information on the following topics: Group instruction; program planning; strategy; tennis for the older adult; tournaments, rules, regulations and organization; tennis facilities; tennis fitness and health; history of tennis.

To order a list of their publications, please write to: Publications Department, USTA Education & Research Center, 729 Alexander Road, Princeton, New Jersey 08540.